EDGE
BOOKS

SUPER COBRA ATTACK HELICOPTERS

The AH-IW

by Michael and Gladys Green

WITHDRAWN

Mankato, Minnesota

Edge Books are published by Capstone Press,
151 Good Counsel Drive, P.O. Box 669, Mankato, Minnesota 56002.
www.capstonepress.com

Library of Congress Cataloging-in-Publication Data
Green, Michael, 1952–
    Super Cobra attack helicopters: the AH-1W / by Michael and Gladys Green.
    p. cm.—(Edge books. War machines)
    Includes bibliographical references and index.
    ISBN 0-7368-3779-5 (hardcover)
    1. Huey Cobra (Helicopter)—Juvenile literature. I. Green, Gladys, 1954–
II. Title. III. Edge Books, war machines.
UG1232.A88G74 2005
623.74'63—dc22   2004012157

Summary: Describes the AH-1W Super Cobra helicopter, including its history,
equipment, weapons, tactics, and future use.

Editorial Credits
Angie Kaelberer, editor; Jason Knudson, set designer; Patrick D. Dentinger, book designer;
    Ted Williams, illustrator; Jo Miller, photo researcher; Scott Thoms, photo editor

Photo Credits
Bell Helicopter Textron Inc., 27, 29
Corbis/Douglas Peebles, 7; George Hall, 8
DVIC/CPL E. M. Thorne, 21; PH2 Stover, 9
Getty Images Inc., 6; AFP Photo/USMC, cover
Photo by Ted Carlson/Fotodynamics, 5, 11, 12, 13, 14, 17, 18–19, 22, 25

**Capstone Press thanks Hank Perry, LTC, USMC (Ret.), Bell Helicopter, Business
Development, Fort Worth, Texas, for his assistance with this book.**

1 2 3 4 5 6 10 09 08 07 06 05

Table of Contents

CHAPTER 1

The Super Cobra in Action

A dozen enemy tanks hide among the ruins of a small town in an enemy country. Soldiers behind the tanks plan to attack a nearby U.S. Marine Corps infantry unit. As the Marines get closer to the town, the enemy tanks open fire. The Marines take cover. They fire missiles at the tanks.

The enemy soldiers rush out to attack the Marines. The Marine commander calls for air support on the radio. Two AH-1W Super Cobra helicopter gunships quickly come to the rescue.

The Super Cobra gunships open fire with their 20 mm automatic cannons. As the shells land around them, the enemy soldiers run away. The Super Cobras then shoot Hellfire antitank missiles at the enemy tanks. The tanks explode in flames. The Marines continue safely.

The AH-1W Super Cobra is armed with antitank missiles.

LEARN ABOUT:

The AH-1W in battle

Fast gunships

Missions

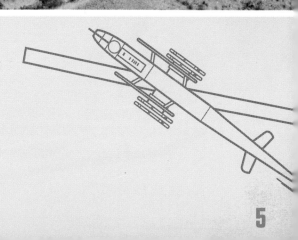

Early Gunships

During the Vietnam War (1954–1975), the military needed helicopter gunships to protect its transport helicopters. The lightly armed transport helicopters moved soldiers, weapons, and supplies. The UH-1 Iroquois was the most common of these transport helicopters. The military called this helicopter the "Huey."

The UH-1 Iroquois was known as the Huey.

Early in the war, the Army and Marines changed some of their transport helicopters into gunships by adding weapons. These early gunships flew slowly because their weapons were so heavy. The military needed a fast gunship that could carry many weapons.

Bell Helicopter developed a helicopter that filled that need. It was called the AH-1G Huey Cobra. The AH-1G was armed with rockets, machine guns, and grenade launchers. It entered service in Vietnam in 1967.

Marine Corps Use

In 1969, the Marines ordered 67 of the Army's AH-1G Huey Cobra gunships. Marine leaders named the new helicopter the AH-1J Sea Cobra. The Sea Cobra had two engines and a larger machine gun than the Huey Cobra did.

The Marines soon found they needed a helicopter able to carry larger loads of weapons during hot weather. This need resulted in the AH-1T Sea Cobra. The Marines began using the AH-1T in 1978.

Bell began making an upgraded version of the AH-1T Sea Cobra in 1986. The new model is the AH-1W Super Cobra. It has more powerful engines and advanced electronics.

The Super Cobra performs many jobs for the Marine Corps. It helps collect information about enemies. It can destroy enemy tanks. The Super Cobra marks targets for jet attack aircraft. It also acts as an armed escort for transport helicopters.

The AH-1W is an improved version of the AH-1T.

CHAPTER 2

Inside the Super Cobra

Two officer pilots make up the Super Cobra's crew. The pilot in command normally flies the helicopter. The copilot/gunner shoots the helicopter's guns and missiles.

In most helicopters, the pilot and copilot sit next to each other. But the Super Cobra is only about 3 feet (1 meter) wide. Its narrow width makes the helicopter harder to see and shoot down during head-on attacks.

The Super Cobra's pilot sits behind the copilot. The pilot's seat is raised slightly. The seat height allows the pilot to see over the copilot's head.

Both crew members wear helmets with a built-in intercom system so they can talk to each other while in flight. The helmets have sensors to see, aim, and shoot at enemy targets.

LEARN ABOUT:

Crew members

Flares and chaff systems

Night missions

Equipment and Controls

To shoot at targets, the copilot uses a telescopic sight unit (TSU). It works like a powerful telescope. With the TSU, the copilot sees targets 13 times clearer than with the naked eye.

The pilot's seat has more gauges than the copilot's seat.

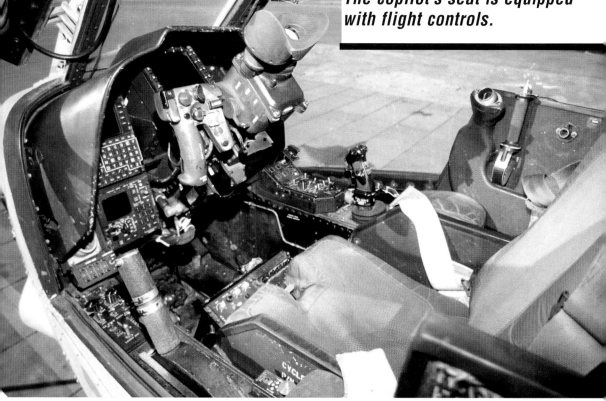

The copilot's seat is equipped with flight controls.

Both crew members can do each other's jobs. The pilot has a Head-Up Display (HUD). This device allows the pilot to fire weapons and fly the aircraft at the same time without looking at the gauges. The copilot also has a set of flight controls.

Flares protect the Super Cobra from enemy missiles.

Defense Systems

Machine guns and automatic cannons are the most common weapons used against the Super Cobra. The Super Cobra's armor protects it from most machine gun bullets. The rotor blades on the Super Cobra can withstand 23 mm automatic cannon fire.

The Super Cobra also has a protection system against heat-seeking missiles. This type of missile has a sensor in its nose. The sensor guides the missile to the heat given off by the helicopter's engines. When the missile gets close to the Super Cobra, the crew releases hot, bright objects called flares. The missile chases after the flares instead of the helicopter.

A chaff dispensing system protects the Super Cobra from radar-guided missiles. When a radar-guided missile comes near the helicopter, the crew releases the chaff. These small metal strips reflect radar waves. This action keeps the missile from finding its target.

Sensors

The Super Cobra sometimes performs missions at night and in bad weather. For these missions, the helicopter has a night targeting system (NTS) on its telescopic sight unit. The NTS includes a forward-looking infrared (FLIR) system, a laser range finder, and a laser designator.

The FLIR system detects heat in objects on the ground at night. This information appears on a screen inside the Super Cobra's cockpit.

The Super Cobra uses the laser range finder to find the distance to a target. The crew aims an invisible laser beam at the target. The laser hits the target and bounces back to the range finder. A computer measures the time the laser took to reach the target and return to the Super Cobra.

The gunship's laser designators can be used against tanks and other targets. The laser designator uses laser light reflecting off targets to guide antitank Hellfire missiles. These missiles have sensors that look for the reflected laser light. The missiles use the light to spot and destroy the targets.

The FLIR system is on the front of the Super Cobra.

AHI-W Super Cobra

Function:	Attack helicopter gunship
Manufacturer:	Bell Helicopter Textron Inc.
Date First Deployed:	1986
Length:	58 feet (17.7 meters)
Body Width:	3.2 feet (1 meter)
Height:	13.7 feet (4.2 meters)
Rotor Diameter:	48 feet (14.6 meters)
Engines:	Two T700 GE-401 gas turbines
Top Speed:	169 miles (272 kilometers) per hour
Range:	294 miles (473 kilometers)
Maximum Altitude:	18,700 feet (5,700 meters)
Weapons:	M197 20 mm automatic cannon; TOW, Hellfire, and Sidewinder missiles; Zuni rockets; FFARs

1 Tail rotor

2 Hellfire missiles

3 Rotor blade

4 Rotor mast

5 FLIR

6 20 mm cannon

CHAPTER 3

Weapons and Tactics

The AH-1W Super Cobra carries several weapons. Its main weapon is an M197 three-barrel 20 mm automatic cannon. It also can carry guided missiles and unguided rockets.

The M197 is used against lightly armored vehicles and other targets. The M197 fires from a chin turret. This rotating weapon holder is on the front of the Super Cobra. Each round fired contains a small explosive charge.

Guided Missiles

The Super Cobra carries two types of guided antitank missiles. One missile is the Tube-launched, Optically-tracked, Wire command-link guided missile system (TOW). The other is the laser-guided Hellfire missile.

LEARN ABOUT:

Cannons

Missiles

Rockets

The TOW has two thin wires attached to it. Flight commands pass along the two wires and guide the missile to its target. The copilot tracks the target through the TSU. The TOW missile then flies to the target. The missile can hit targets as far away as 2 miles (3.2 kilometers).

The Hellfire uses a laser designator to locate enemy targets. Hellfire missiles have a range of about 5 miles (8 kilometers).

The Sidewinder guided air-to-air missile protects the Super Cobra from enemy aircraft. The Sidewinder uses a seeker head in its nose to find its target. The seeker head searches for the hot engine exhaust of the enemy aircraft. The Sidewinder has a range of about 10 miles (16 kilometers).

Unguided Rockets

The Super Cobra carries two types of unguided rockets. These are Folding Fin Aircraft Rockets (FFAR) and Zuni rockets.

Both rockets are area weapons. They are not as accurate as machine guns and guided missiles. Instead, they cover a target area with many hits. Both rockets can hit targets within about 5 miles (8 kilometers).

Super Cobras carry Hellfire missiles and FFAR rockets.

Tactics

Helicopters fly much slower than jets. Helicopters' slow speed makes them easier targets for enemy weapons. To overcome this problem, the Super Cobra flies low to the ground. The Super Cobra uses trees, hills, and buildings as cover.

The Super Cobra stays behind cover as it sneaks up on a target. Once the target is in range, it pops up and fires its weapons. Before the enemy can return fire, the Super Cobra drops behind cover. It then moves to a new firing position.

The Super Cobra flies low to the ground.

CHAPTER 4

The Future

The AH-1W models will reach the end of their service life by 2014. Instead of buying new helicopters, the Marine Corps is improving 180 of its Super Cobras. The new version is the AH-1Z Super Cobra.

The first test model of the AH-1Z flew in December 2000. Bell Helicopter Textron built the first production AH-1Z Super Cobras in 2004.

Major Design

The AH-1Z has a four-bladed rotor system. The four blades provide more lift than the two blades on the AH-1W. This extra lift allows the AH-1Z to fly faster and higher. The lift also helps the AH-1Z carry more weapons than the AH-1W can.

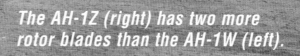

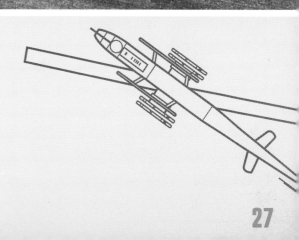

LEARN ABOUT:

AH-1Z

Rotor system

Built-in sights

Marine Corps leaders wanted the AH-1Z to be safer than the AH-1W. The AH-1Z has seats and landing gear that absorb impact during landings or crashes. It has self-sealing fuel tanks that help prevent fires.

Improved Equipment

The AH-1Z also will be more effective on the battlefield. It has a target sight system (TSS). This system helps the AH-1Z spot enemy targets at greater distances than the AH-1W can.

On the AH-1Z, both the pilot and copilot wear helmets with a built-in sight. They can aim the cannon just by looking at a target.

The Super Cobra has served the Marine Corps for many years. The gunships have performed missions in conditions ranging from arctic cold to desert heat. The new AH-1Z will continue to help the U.S. Marines protect the nation and the world.

The AH-1Z can hit more distant targets than the AH-1W can.

Glossary

armor (AR-mur)—a heavy metal layer that protects against bullets or bombs

chaff (CHAF)—strips of metal foil dropped by an aircraft to confuse enemy radar

laser beam (LAY-zur BEEM)—a narrow, intense beam of light

missile (MISS-uhl)—an explosive weapon that can fly long distances

radar (RAY-dar)—equipment that uses radio waves to find and guide objects

rotor (ROH-tur)—machinery that spins a set of rotating blades; rotors allow helicopter pilots to lift or steer an aircraft.

sensor (SEN-sur)—an instrument that detects physical changes in the environment

turret (TUR-it)—a rotating part on top of an aircraft that holds a weapon

Read More

Abramovitz, Melissa. *U.S. Marine Corps at War*. On the Front Lines. Mankato, Minn.: Capstone Press, 2002.

Benson, Michael. *The U.S. Marine Corps*. U.S. Armed Forces. Minneapolis: Lerner, 2005.

Cooper, Jason. *U.S. Marine Corps*. Fighting Forces. Vero Beach, Fla.: Rourke, 2004.

Internet Sites

FactHound offers a safe, fun way to find Internet sites related to this book. All of the sites on FactHound have been researched by our staff.

Here's how:

1. Visit *www.facthound.com*
2. Type in this special code **0736837795** for age-appropriate sites. Or enter a search word related to this book for a more general search.
3. Click on the **Fetch It** button.

FactHound will fetch the best sites for you!

Index